DR. BOB'S AMAZING WORLD OF ANIMALS

ANIMALS

POLAR BEARS

By Ruth Owen

WINDMILL BOOKS
New York

Published in 2012 by Windmill Books, An Imprint of Rosen Publishing
29 East 21st Street, New York, NY 10010

Copyright © 2012 Ruby Tuesday Books Ltd

Adaptations to North American edition © 2012 Windmill Books, An Imprint of Rosen Publishing

Editor for Ruby Tuesday Books Ltd: Mark J. Sachner
U.S. Editor: Sara Antill
Designer: Trudi Webb

Photo Credits: Cover, 4–5, 7, 8–9, 10–11, 12–13, 14–15, 16–17, 18, 22–23, 24–25, 27, 28, 30 © Shutterstock; 19 © Superstock; 20–21, 29 © FLPA.

Library of Congress Cataloging-in-Publication Data

Owen, Ruth, 1967–
  Polar bears / By Ruth Owen.
  p. cm. — (Dr. Bob's amazing world of animals)
  Includes index.
  ISBN 978-1-61533-546-6 (library binding) —
  ISBN 978-1-61533-552-7 (pbk.) —
  ISBN 978-1-61533-553-4 (6-pack)
  1. Polar bear—Juvenile literature. I.
Title.
QL737.C27O965 2012
599.786—dc23

                         2011020943

Manufactured in the United States of America

CPSIA Compliance Information: Batch #RTW2102WM: For Further Information contact Windmill Books, New York, New York at 1-866-478-0556

Contents

The Polar Bear

Welcome to my amazing world of animals. Today, we are in the cold, icy world of the polar bear!

Let's investigate...

Hank's
WOOF OF WISDOM!

The polar bear is the largest **predator** that lives on land.

Scientists use a very old language called Latin to give animals scientific names. The polar bear's scientific name is *Ursus maritimus*. It means "sea bear."

Polar bears are strong swimmers.

A polar bear was recorded swimming in the ocean for 100 miles (161 km)!

The Land of the Polar Bear

Polar bears live near the **North Pole**. This part of the world is called the Arctic.

A large area of the Arctic Ocean is always frozen. This is called the polar ice cap.

Polar ice cap

Icy land

Russia

North Pole

Greenland

Arctic Ocean

Alaska (U.S.)

Canada

Pacific Ocean

Atlantic Ocean

United States

The pink area on the map is where polar bears live.

In winter, more of the ocean freezes and the ice cap gets bigger. It joins up with the edges of the icy land!

- United States (Alaska)
- Canada
- Russia
- Greenland
- Norway

Icy sea and land

Hank's WOOF OF WISDOM!

In the land of the polar bear, it can be colder than the inside of your freezer!

Polar Bear Bodies

Polar bears look white, but their fur is actually see-through!

When light hits the see-through fur, it makes the fur look white.

Polar bears have black skin and black tongues.

Say AAAHHH, please.

Bear Size Chart

A polar bear is huge compared to a human!

Adult male
polar bear

Weight =
up to 1,200
pounds
(544 kg)

Up to 10 feet (3 m) long

Weight =
up to 650
pounds
(295 kg)

Adult female
polar bear

Up to 6.5 feet (2 m) long

The biggest polar bear ever recorded weighed
2,209 pounds (1,002 kg). That's the same as 12 adult men!

How Do Polar Bears Stay Warm?

Polar bears have two layers of fur. They have a top layer of thick, oily fur and an undercoat of short, woolly fur.

Polar bear bodies also have a thick layer of fat, called **blubber**.

Polar bear bodies are so good at staying warm that the bears can actually get too hot!

Hot polar bears roll in the snow to cool off!

Polar bears have fur on the bottoms of their feet. This helps them grip the ice.

A polar bear's foot is as big as a dinner plate!

Bear Breakfast

A polar bear's favorite food is seals.

An adult polar bear will eat a seal's blubber. That leaves the rest of the seal for other animals, such as arctic foxes, to eat.

A bear will eat up to 100 pounds (45 kg) of blubber in one meal.

Polar bears can smell food that is about 2 miles (3 km) away!

Polar Bear Menu

Polar bears also eat these animals.

Beluga Whales

Walruses

Beached Whales

Hank's WOOF OF WISDOM!

If bears cannot find large animals to eat, they will eat birds, eggs, grass, and even seaweed!

Hunting Skills

Polar bears hunt for seals on the frozen Arctic Ocean.

Seals live in the ocean, under the ice.
They make air holes in the ice and come to the surface to breathe.

Yikes!

A polar bear will wait by an air hole.
It might have to wait for hours!
When a seal pops up to breathe, the bear uses its huge paws to hit and kill the seal.

When seals rest on the ice, polar bears creep up on them. Then, they attack!

A polar bear's white fur helps **camouflage** it against the ice.

Come Over for Dinner

Adult polar bears spend most of their time alone. Sometimes they will get together to share some food.

One bear may find a large meal such as a dead whale. Other bears will want to share it.

It's important that a bear shows good manners
if it wants to share another bear's food.
The bear must stay low to the ground
and walk around the food.
Then, it must ask to share the food
by gently touching noses with
the other bear.

Hank's
WOOF OF WISDOM!

A scientist studying
polar bears once saw
100 polar bears sharing
a whale!

Moms and Babies

Let's find out about polar bear families!

Polar bear babies are called cubs.

Female bears start to have cubs when they are between 4 and 8 years old.

First, a male and a female bear meet and **mate**.

In late October or early November, the pregnant female bear digs a den under the snow. She stays in the den all winter.

The den is under here. It is about 3 feet (1 m) high and 6 feet (2 m) long.

Female bear

In January or February, her cubs are born!

Meet Some Cubs!

Inside her den, the mother polar bear gives birth to one, two, or three cubs.

Newborn cubs are about 14 inches (35 cm) long.
They are blind and have no teeth.
The mother bear feeds the cubs milk from her body.

A mother polar bear's huge body keeps her cubs warm.

These cubs are 3 months old.

The cubs grow fast. In March or April, it is time for them to leave the den.

The mother bear has not had anything to eat or drink all winter. She is very hungry when she leaves the den.

Growing Up

The cubs grow fast! They like to play in the snow.

The mother bear keeps watch for danger at all times.

Wolves and hungry male bears will sometimes eat cubs.

Mother bears lick their cubs to keep them clean. They cuddle them, too!

A milk break

A swimming lesson

The cubs stay with their mother for 2 to 3 years. They learn how to hunt by watching her.

Hank's
WOOF OF WISDOM!

During their first year, cubs are known as COYs. "COYs" stands for "cubs of the year."

Polar Bears in Danger

There are between 20,000 and 25,000 polar bears in the Arctic. The bears are in danger, though!

In summer, the sea ice melts. The bears need to be on the ice to hunt for seals.

They will try to swim from the land to the ice. Sometimes it's too far, though.

Some bears spend the summer very hungry.

Scientists have been measuring the sea ice. Every year, the amount of sea ice is getting smaller. The ice is melting because our planet is getting warmer.

If all the sea ice melts, the bears will not be able to hunt seals. The polar bears will die.

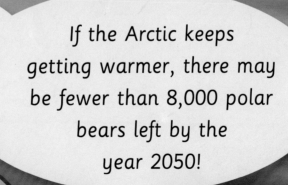

Hank's
WOOF OF WISDOM!

If the Arctic keeps getting warmer, there may be fewer than 8,000 polar bears left by the year 2050!

Polar Bears Need Ice

The Arctic is getting warmer because of **climate change**.

People burn fuel to power cars or make electricity.

Gases

Burning fuel puts gases into the air.

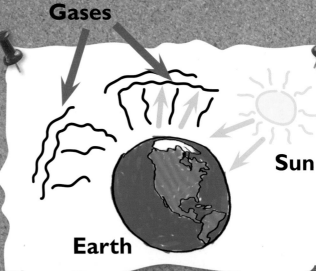

Electricity plant

The gases gather high above the Earth. The gases trap too much heat from the Sun.

Gases

Sun

Earth

This changes the **climate**. Earth gets hotter. The ice at the North Pole and South Pole melts.

Hank's WOOF OF WISDOM!

If you switch off a light or walk instead of taking the car, you will be saving energy. When you save energy, fewer gases go into the air, and you will be helping the polar bears.

Bear Tracking

One way that scientists study polar bears is by tracking them.

A bear is put to sleep using a drug in a dart gun. A satellite collar is then put on the bear.

The collar uses satellites to send information to scientists who study polar bears.

Only female bears can wear satellite collars. A male bear's neck is thicker than its head so the collar will fall off!

The scientists track where the bear hunts and how much time it spends in the ocean.

The more we know about polar bears, the more we will be able to help them!

Glossary

blubber (BLUH-ber)
Thick fat that keeps animals living in cold places or in the ocean warm. Polar bears, seals, and whales all have blubber.

camouflage (KA-muh-flahj)
To hide an animal or allow it to blend in with its surroundings.

climate (KLY-mut)
The different types of weather and temperatures over many years.

climate change (KLY-mut CHAYNJ)
The slow warming of planet Earth. Climate change is happening because gases from burning fuels such as coal and oil gather high above the planet and trap the Sun's heat.

mate (MAYT)
When a male and a female animal get together to produce young.

North Pole (NORTH POHL)
The northermost point on Earth.

predator (PREH-duh-ter)
An animal that hunts and kills other animals for food.

Dr. Bob's Fast Fact Board

The Inuit people of the Arctic call the polar bear Nanuk.

In the summer it is light 24 hours a day in the Arctic. In winter, it is dark, day and night.

A newborn polar bear cub weighs about 1 pound (0.5 kg).

After eating, a polar bear will take a bath in the ocean. It will rub itself in snow to dry off.

A polar bear can run at 25 miles an hour (40 km/h). It only runs for a short time, however, so it does not overheat!

Web Sites

For Web resources related to the subject of this book, go to: **www.windmillbooks.com/weblinks** and select this book's title.

Read More

Miller, Sara Swan. *Polar Bears of the Arctic.* Brrr! Polar Animals. New York: PowerKids Press, 2009.

Newman, Mark. *Polar Bears.* New York: Henry Holt and Co., 2010.

Rosing, Norbert and Elizabeth Carney. *Face to Face with Polar Bears.* Face to Face with Animals. Des Moines, IA: National Geographic Children's Books, 2009.

Index